'A glass
a lover lovely as
The moon . . .'

HAFEZ
Born *c.* 1317, Shiraz, Iran
Died 1390, Shiraz, Iran

All poems taken from *Faces of Love: Hafez and the Poets of Shiraz*, introduced and translated by Dick Davies.

HAFEZ IN PENGUIN CLASSICS
Faces of Love: Hafez and the Poets of Shiraz

HAFEZ

The nightingales are drunk

Translated by
Dick Davies

PENGUIN BOOKS

PENGUIN CLASSICS

Published by the Penguin Group
Penguin Books Ltd, 80 Strand, London WC2R ORL, England
Penguin Group (USA) Inc., 375 Hudson Street, New York, New York 10014, USA
Penguin Group (Canada), 90 Eglinton Avenue East, Suite 700, Toronto, Ontario,
Canada M4P 2Y3 (a division of Pearson Penguin Canada Inc.)
Penguin Ireland, 25 St Stephen's Green, Dublin 2, Ireland
(a division of Penguin Books Ltd)
Penguin Group (Australia), 707 Collins Street, Melbourne, Victoria 3008, Australia
(a division of Pearson Australia Group Pty Ltd)
Penguin Books India Pvt Ltd, 11 Community Centre, Panchsheel Park,
New Delhi – 110 017, India
Penguin Group (NZ), 67 Apollo Drive, Rosedale, Auckland 0632, New Zealand
(a division of Pearson New Zealand Ltd)
Penguin Books (South Africa) (Pty) Ltd, Block D, Rosebank Office Park,
181 Jan Smuts Avenue, Parktown North, Gauteng 2193, South Africa

Penguin Books Ltd, Registered Offices: 80 Strand, London WC2R ORL, England

www.penguin.com

First published by Mage Press 2012
This selection published in Penguin Classics 2015
001

Translation copyright © Mage Publishers, 2012
The moral right of the translator has been asserted

Set in 9.5/13 pt Baskerville 10 Pro
Typeset by Jouve (UK), Milton Keynes
Printed in Great Britain by Clays Ltd, St Ives plc

A CIP catalogue record for this book is available from the British Library

ISBN: 978-0-141-98026-3

www.greenpenguin.co.uk

Contents

A black mole graced his face   1

Ah, God forbid that I
    relinquish wine   2

Come, tell me what it is that
    I have gained   4

Dear friends   6

For years my heart inquired
    of me   8

Go mind your own business,
    preacher!   10

Good news! The days of grief
    and pain   12

I see no love in anyone   14

I've known the pains of love's
    frustration – ah, don't ask!   16

Last night I saw the angels   17

Life's garden flourishes   19

May I remember always   21

Mild breeze of morning   23

Moslcms, timc was I had a
    heart –   25

My body's dust is as a veil   27

My heart, good fortune is the
    only friend   29

Of all the roses in the world   31

The musky morning breeze   33

The nightgales are drunk   35

Though wine is pleasurable   37

To give up wine, and human
    beauty?   39

What does life give me in
    the end but sorrow?   41

What memories!   42

Where is the news we'll meet   44

Flirtatious games, and youth   46

With wine beside a gently
    flowing brook – this is best   48

A black mole graced his face; he Stripped, and shone
    Incomparable in splendor as the moon;
He was so slim his heart was visible,
As if clear water sluiced a granite stone.

Ah, god forbid that I relinquish wine
      When roses are in season;
How could I do this when I'm someone who
      Makes such a show of Reason?

Where's a musician, so that I can give
      The profit I once found
In self-control and knowledge for a flute's songs,
      And a lute's sweet sound?

The endless arguments within the schools –
      Whatever they might prove –
Sickened my heart; I'll give a little time
      To wine now, and to love.

Where is the shining messenger of dawn
      That I might now complain
To my good fortune's harbinger of this
      Long night of lonely pain?

But when did time keep faith with anyone?
      Bring wine, and I'll recall
The tales of kings, of Jamshid and Kavus,
      And how time took them all.

I'm not afraid of sins recorded in
      My name – I'll roll away

A hundred such accounts, by His benevolence
    And grace, on Judgment Day.

This lent soul, that the Friend once gave into
    Hafez's care, I'll place
Within His hands again, on that day when
    I see Him face to face.

Come, tell me what it is that
     I have gained
   From loving you,
Apart from losing all the faith I had
   And knowledge too?

Though longing for you scatters on the wind
   All my life's work,
Still, by the dust on your dear feet, I have
   Kept faith with you.

And even though I'm just a tiny mote
   In love's great kingdom,
I'm one now with the sun, before your face,
   In loving you.

Bring wine! In all my life I've never known
   A corner where
I could sit snugly, safely, and enjoy
   Contentment too.

And, if you're sensible, don't ply me with
   Advice; your words
Are wasted on me, and the reason is
   I'm drunk; it's true!

How can I not feel hopeless shame when I
    Am near my love?
What service could I offer him? What could
    I say or do?

Hafez is burned, but his bewitching love
    Has yet to say,
'Hafez, I wounded you, and here's the balm
    I send for you.'

Dear friends, that friend with whom we once
      Caroused at night –
His willing services to us
      And our delight . . . remember this.

And in your joy, when tinkling bells
      And harps are there,
Include within your songs the sound
      Of love's despair . . . remember this.

When wine bestows a smile upon
      Your server's face,
Keep in your songs, for lovers then,
      A special place . . . remember this.

So all that you have hoped for is
      Fulfilled at last?
All that we talked of long ago,
      Deep in the past . . . remember this.

When love is faithful, and it seems
      Nothing can hurt you,
Know that the world is faithless still
      And will desert you . . . remember this.

If Fortune's horse bolts under you,
      Then call to mind
Your riding whip, and see your friends
      Aren't left behind . . . remember this.

O you, who dwell in splendor now,
      Glorious and proud,
Pity Hafez, your threshold's where
      His face is bowed . . . remember this.

For years my heart inquired of me
    Where Jamshid's sacred cup might be,
And what was in its own possession
    It asked from strangers, constantly;
Begging the pearl that's slipped its shell
    From lost souls wandering by the sea.

Last night I took my troubles to
    The Magian sage whose keen eyes see
A hundred answers in the wine;
    Laughing, he showed the cup to me –
I asked him, 'When was this cup
    That shows the world's reality

Handed to you?' He said, 'The day
    Heaven's vault of lapis lazuli
Was raised, and marvelous things took place
    By Intellect's divine decree,
And Moses' miracles were made
    And Sameri's apostacy.'

He added then, 'That friend they hanged
    High on the looming gallows tree –
His sin was that he spoke of things
    Which should be pondered secretly;

The page of truth his heart enclosed
  Was annotated publicly.

But if the Holy Ghost once more
  Should lend his aid to us, we'd see
Others perform what Jesus did –
  Since in his heart-sick anguish he
Was unaware that God was there
  And called His name out ceaselessly.'

I asked him next, 'And beauties' curls
  That tumble down so sinuously,
What do they mean? Whence do they come?'
  'Hafez,' the sage replied to me,
'Their source is your distracted heart
  That asks these questions constantly.'

Go, mind your own business,
    preacher! what's all
    This hullabaloo?
My heart has left the road you travel, but
    What's that to you?

Until my lips are played on like a flute
    By his lips' beauty,
My ears can only hear as wind the world's
    Advice on duty –

God made him out of nothing, and within
    His being's state
There is a mystery no being's skill
    Can penetrate.

The beggar in your street disdains eight heavens
    For what he's given;
The captive in your chains is free of this world
    And of heaven;

And even though the drunkenness of love
    Has ruined me,
My being's built upon those ruins for
    Eternity.

My heart, don't whine so often that your friend's
    Unjust to you;
This is the fate he's given you, and this
    Is justice too.

Be off with you, Hafez! Enough of all
    These tales you tell;
I've heard these tales and fables many times;
    I know them well.

Good news! the days of grief and pain
                won't stay like this –
As others went, these won't remain
                or stay like this.

Though my belovèd thinks of me
                as dirt and dust,
My rival's status, and her trust,
                won't stay like this.

And though the doorman wields his sword
                against us all,
No rank remains immutable
                or stays like this.

When good or bad come, why give thanks,
                and why complain?
Since what is written won't remain
                or stay like this.

They say when Jamshid reigned, 'Bring wine'
                was his court's song,
'Since even Jamshid won't live long,
                or stay like this.'

And if you're wealthy help the poor,
                since, be assured,

The gold and silver that you hoard
        won't stay like this!

O candle, prize the moth's love now
        and hold it fast –
When dawn arrives it cannot last
        or stay like this.

In words of gold they've written on
        the emerald sky,
'Only compassion does not die
        but stays like this.'

Do not despair of love, Hafez;
        it can't be true
The heartlessness she's shown to you
        will stay like this.

I see no love in anyone,
Where, then, have all the lovers gone?
And when did all our friendship end,
And what's become of every friend?

Life's water's muddied now, and where
Is Khezr to guide us from despair?
The rose has lost its coloring,
What's happened to the breeze of spring?

A hundred thousand flowers appear
But no birds sing for them to hear –
Thousands of nightingales are dumb:
Where are they now? Why don't they come?

For years no rubies have been found
In stony mines deep underground;
When will the sun shine forth again?
Where are the clouds brimful of rain?

Who thinks of drinking now? No one.
Where have the roistering drinkers gone?
This was a town of lovers once,
Of kindness and benevolence,

And when did kindness end? What brought
The sweetness of our town to naught?

The ball of generosity
Lies on the field for all to see –

No rider comes to strike it; where
Is everyone who should be there?
Silence, Hafez, since no one knows
The secret ways that heaven goes;

Who is it that you're asking how
The heavens are revolving now?

I've known the pains of love's
    frustration – ah, don't ask!
I've drained the dregs of separation – ah, don't ask!

I've been about the world and found at last
A lover worthy of my adoration – ah, don't ask!

So that my tears now lay the dust before
Her door in constant supplication – ah, don't ask!

Last night, with my own ears, I heard such words
Fall from her in our conversation – ah, don't ask!

You bite your lip at me? The lip I bite
Is all delicious delectation! – ah, don't ask!

Without you, in this beggarly poor hut,
I have endured such desolation – ah, don't ask!

Lost on love's road, like Hafez, I've attained
A stage . . . but stop this speculation – ah, don't ask!

Last night I saw the angels
    tapping at the wine-shop's door,
And kneading Adam's dust,
    and molding it as cups for wine;

And, where I sat beside the road,
    these messengers of heaven
Gave me their wine to drink,
    so that their drunkenness was mine.

The heavens could not bear
    the heavy trust they had been given,
And lots were cast, and crazed
    Hafez's name received the sign.

Forgive the seventy-two
    competing factions – all their tales
Mean that the Truth is what
    they haven't seen, and can't define!

But I am thankful that there's peace
    between Him now, and me;
In celebration of our pact
    the houris drink their wine –

And fire is not what gently smiles
    from candles' flames, it's what

Annihilates the flocking moths
   that flutter round His shrine.

No one has drawn aside the veil
   of Thought as Hafez has,
Or combed the curls of Speech
   as his sharp pen has, line by line.

Life's garden flourishes when your
      Bright countenance is here.
Come back! Without your face's bloom
      The spring has left the year.

If tears course down like raindrops now,
      It's no surprise, it's right –
My life's flashed by in longing for you
      As lightning splits the night.

Seize these few moments while we've still
      Time for our promised meeting,
Since no one knows what life will bring
      And life, my dear, is fleeting.

How long shall we enjoy our dawns'
      Sweet sleep, our morning wine?
Wake up, and think of this! Since life's
      Not yours for long, or mine.

She passed by yesterday, but gave
      Me not a glance, not one;
My wretched heart, you've witnessed nothing
      As life's passed by, and gone.

But those whose lives are centered on
      Your lovely mouth confess

No other thoughts than this, and think
      Nothing of Nothingness.

An ambush waits on every side
      Wherever we might tread,
And so life's rider rides slack-reined,
      Giving his horse its head.

I've lived my life without a life –
      Don't be surprised at this;
Who counts an absence as a life
      When life is what you miss?

Speak Hafez! On the world's page trace
      Your poems' narrative;
The words your pen writes will have life
      When you no longer live.

May I remember always when
   Your glance in secrecy met mine,
And in my face your love was like
   A visibly reflected sign.

May I remember always when
   Your chiding eyes were like my death
And your sweet lips restored my life
   Like Jesus's reviving breath.

May I remember always when
   We drank our wine as darkness died,
My friend and I, alone at dawn,
   Though God was there too, at our side.

May I remember always when
   Your face was pleasure's flame, and my
Poor fluttering heart was like a moth
   That's singed and is about to die.

May I remember always when
   The company that we were in
Was so polite, and when it seemed
   Only the wine would wink and grin!

May I remember always when
   Our goblet laughed with crimson wine –

What tales passed back and forth between
    Your ruby lips, my dear, and mine!

May I remember always when
    I was a canopy unfurled
That shaded you, and you were like
    The new moon riding through the world.

May I remember always when
    I sat and drank in wine-shops where
What I can't find in mosques today
    Accompanied the drinkers there.

May I remember always when
    The jewels of verse Hafez selected
Were set out properly by you,
    Arranged in order, and corrected.

Mild breeze of morning, gently tell
  That errant, elegant gazelle
She's made me wander far and wide
  About the hills and countryside.

My sugar-lipped, sweet girl – oh, may
  You live forever and a day! –
Where is your kindness? Come now, show it
  To your sweet-talking parrot-poet.

My rose, does vanity restrain you?
  Does beauty's arrogance detain you
From seeking out this nightingale
  Who wildly sings, to no avail?

With gentleness and kindness lies
  The surest way to win the wise,
Since birds that have become aware
  Of ropes and traps are hard to snare.

When you sit safely with your love,
  Sipping your wine, be mindful of
Those struggling lovers who still stray,
  Wind-tossed, upon their weary way.

I don't know why she isn't here,
  Why her tall presence won't appear,

Or why the full moon of her face,
   And her black eyes, avoid this place.

No fault can be imputed to
   Your beauty's excellence, or you,
Except that there is not a trace
   Of truth or kindness in your face.

When Hafez speaks, it's no surprise
   If Venus dances in the skies
And leads across the heavens' expanse
   Lord Jesus in the whirling dance.

Moslems, time was I had a heart –
        a good one too,
When problems came we'd talk, and I'd
        know what to do;

And if I tumbled in grief's whirlpool
        my heart was sure
To give me hope that soon enough
        I'd reach the shore –

A sympathetic, generous heart,
        a heart prepared
To help out any noble soul,
        a heart that cared.

This heart was lost to me within
        my lover's street;
God, what a place! – where I succumbed
        to sweet deceit.

There is no faultless art – we all
        fall short somehow,
But what poor beggar's more deprived
        than I am now?

Have pity on this wretched soul
        and sympathize

With one who once upon a time
       was strong and wise.

Since love has taught me how to talk,
       each little phrase
Of mine is cried up everywhere
       and showered with praise –

But don't call Hafez witty, wise,
       intelligent;
I've seen Hafez, I know him well;
       he's ignorant.

My body's dust is as a veil
    Spread out to hide
My soul – happy that moment when
    It's drawn aside!

To cage a songbird with so sweet
    A voice is wrong –
I'll fly to paradise's garden
    Where I belong.

But why I've come and whence I came
    Is all unclear –
Alas, to know so little of
    My being here!

How can I make my journey to
    My heavenly home
When I'm confined and cramped within
    This flesh and bone?

If my blood smells of longing, show no
    Astonishment –
Mine is the musk deer's pain as he
    Secretes his scent.

Don't think my golden shirt is like
    A candle's light –

The true flame burns beneath my shirt,
　　Hidden from sight.

Come, and ensure Hafez's being
　　Will disappear –
Since You exist, no one will hear
　　Me say, 'I'm here.'

My heart, good fortune is the only friend
    Going along beside you that you need;
A breeze that's scented with Shiraz's gardens
    Is all the guard to guide you that you need.

Poor wretch, don't leave your lover's home again,
    Don't be in such a hurry to depart –
A corner of our Sufi meeting place,
    The journey in your heart . . . are all you need.

The claims of home, the promises you made
    An ancient friend – these are enough to say
When making your excuses to the travelers
    Who've been along life's way . . . they're all you need.

If grief should leap out from some corner of
    Your stubborn heart and ambush you, confide
Your troubles to our ancient Zoroastrian –
    His precincts will provide . . . you all you need.

Sit yourself down upon the wine-shop's bench
    And take a glass of wine – this is your share
Of all the wealth and glory of the world,
    And what you're given there . . . is all you need.

Let go, and make life easy for yourself,
    Don't strain and struggle, always wanting more;

A glass of wine, a lover lovely as
    The moon – you may be sure . . . they're all you need.

The heavens give the ignorant their head,
    Desire's the only bridle they acknowledge –
Your fault is that you're clever and accomplished,
    And this same sin of knowledge . . . is all you need.

And you require no other prayer, Hafez,
    Than that prayed in the middle of the night;
This and the morning lesson you repeat
    As dawn displays her light . . . are all you need.

Don't look for gifts from others; in both worlds –
    This world, the world that is to come – your king's
Kind bounty, and the Lord's approval, are
    The two essential things . . . they're all you need.

Of all the roses in the world
　　A rosy face . . . is quite enough for me;
Beneath this swaying cypress tree
　　A shady place . . . is quite enough for me.

May hypocrites find somewhere else
　　To cant and prate –
Of all this weighty world, a full
　　Wine-glass's weight . . . is quite enough for me.

They hand out heaven for good deeds!
　　The monastery
Where Magians live is better for
　　A sot like me . . . that's quite enough for me.

Sit by this stream and watch as life
　　Flows swiftly on –
This emblem of the world that's all
　　Too quickly gone . . . is quite enough for me.

See how the world's bazaar pays cash,
　　See the world's pain –
And if you're not content with this
　　World's loss and gain . . . they're quite enough for me.

My friend is here with me – what more
　　Should I desire?

The riches of our talk are all
  That I require . . . they're quite enough for me.

Don't send me from your door, O God,
  To paradise –
For me, to wait here at Your street's
  End will suffice . . . that's quite enough for me.

Hafez, don't rail against your fate!
  Your nature flows,
As does your verse, like water as
  It comes and goes . . . that's quite enough for me.

The musky morning breeze
    Will gently blow again,
Once more the old world will
    Turn young and grow again;

White jasmine will take wine
    From glowing Judas trees,
Narcissi fondly glance
    At shy anemones;

Once more the banished, lovelorn
    Nightingale will bring
His passion to the rose
    And there sublimely sing;

And if I leave the mosque
    For wine, don't sneer at me –
Sermons are long, and time
    Moves on incessantly.

My heart, if you postpone
    Today's enjoyment, who
Will guarantee the cash
    Of happiness to you?

Drink before fasting, drink,
    Don't put your glass down yet –

Since Ramadan draws near
   And pleasure's sun must set.

How sweet the roses are!
   Enjoy them now, for they
As quickly as they bloomed
   Will fall and fade away.

We're all friends here, my boy,
   Sing love songs! Why should you
Sing yet again, 'As that
   Has gone, so this must too'?

You are why Hafez lives –
   But now, within your heart,
Prepare to say farewell,
   Since he too must depart.

The nightingales are drunk, wine-red roses appear,
And, Sufis, all around us, happiness is here;

How firmly, like a rock, Repentance stood! Look how
A wine-glass taps it, and it lies in pieces now . . .

Bring wine! From the sequestered court where we're
    secluded,
Drunk or sober, king or soldier, none will be excluded;

This inn has two doors, and through one we have to go –
What does it matter if the doorway's high or low?

If there's no sorrow there can be no happiness,
And, when the world was made, men knew this, and
        said, 'Yes.'

Rejoice, don't fret at Being and Non-Being; say
That all perfection will be nothingness one day.

The horse that rode the wind, Asef in all his glory,
The language of the birds, are now an ancient story;

They've disappeared upon the wind, and Solomon,
The master of them all, has nothing now they've gone.

Don't rise on feathered wings, don't soar into the skies –
An arrow falls to earth, however far it flies;

How will your pen give thanks, Hafez, now men
    demand
Your verses everywhere, and pass them hand to hand?

Though wine is pleasurable, and though the
    breeze
    Seems soaked in roses, see your harp
Is silent when you drink – because the ears
    Of morals officers are sharp!

If you can find a wine jug and a friend,
    Drink sensibly, and with discretion,
Because the dreadful days we're living through
    Are rife with mischief, and oppression.

See that you hide your wine-cup in your sleeve;
    Your jug's lip sheds its wine, blood-red –
And, in the same way, these cruel times ensure
    Red blood is copiously shed.

We'd better wash away the wine stains from
    Our cloaks with tears of penitence –
Now is the season for sobriety,
    For days of pious abstinence.

The heavens have become a sieve that strains
    Upon us blood, and it is full
Of bloody scraps like royal Khosrow's crown,
    Together with King Kasra's skull.

Don't think that as the heavens turn they'll bring
   A trace of solace or relief;
Their hurtful curvature is through and through
   Made up of wretchedness and grief.

Pars knows the splendor of your verse, Hafez –
   It's made the towns of Eraq glad;
So now's the time to try it out elsewhere –
   Tabriz, perhaps, and then Baghdad.

To give up wine, and human beauty? And to give
  up love?
      No, I won't do it.
A hundred times I said I would; what was I thinking of?
      No, I won't do it.

To say that paradise, its houris, and its shade are more
To me than is the dusty street before my lover's door?
      No, I won't do it.

Sermons, and wise men's words, are signs, and that's
  how we should treat them;
I mouthed such metaphors before, but now – I won't
  repeat them;
      No, I won't do it.

I'll never understand myself, I'll never really know me,
Until I've joined the wine-shop's clientele, and that will
  show me;
      I have to do it.

The preacher told me, 'Give up wine' – contempt was
  in the saying;
'Sure,' I replied. Why should I listen to these
  donkeys braying?
      No, I won't do it.

The sheikh was angry when he told me, 'Give up
    love!' My brother,
There's no end to our arguing about it, so why bother?
        And I won't do it.

My abstinence is this: that when I wink and smile at
    beauty
It won't be from the pulpit in the mosque – I know
    my duty;
        No, I won't do it.

Hafez, good fortune's with the Magian sage, and I
    am sure
I'll never cease to kiss the dust that lies before his door;
        No, I won't do it.

What does life give me in the end but sorrow?
What do love's good and evil send but sorrow?
I've only seen one true companion – pain,
And I have known no faithful friend but sorrow.

What memories! I once lived on
      the street that you lived on,
And to my eyes how bright the dust
      before your doorway shone!

We were a lily and a rose:
      our talk was then so pure
That what was hidden in your heart
      and what I said were one!

And when our hearts discoursed
      with Wisdom's ancient words,
Love's commentary solved each crux
      within our lexicon.

I told my heart that I would never be
      without my friend;
But when our efforts fail, and hearts
      Are weak, what can be done?

Last night, for old times' sake, I saw
      the place where we once drank;
A cask was lying there, its lees
      like blood; mud was its bung.

How much I wandered, asking why
      the pain of parting came –

But Reason was a useless judge,
      and answers? He had none.

And though it's true the turquoise seal
      of Bu Es'haq shone brightly,
His splendid kingdom and his reign
      were all too quickly gone.

Hafez, you've seen a strutting partridge
      whose cry sounds like a laugh –
He's careless of the hawk's sharp claws
      by which he'll be undone.

Where is the news we'll meet, that from
    This life to greet you there   I may arise?
I am a bird from paradise,
    And from this world's cruel snare   I will arise.

Now by my love for you, I swear
    That if you summon me
To be your slave, from all existence
    And its sovereignty   I will arise.

O Lord, make rain fall from Your cloud
    Sent to us as a guide,
Send it before, like scattered dust
    That's wind-blown far and wide,   I will arise.

Sit by my dust with wine and music:
    From my imprisonment
Beneath the ground, within my grave,
    Dancing, drawn by your scent,   I will arise.

Rise now, my love, display your stature,
    Your sweetness, and I'll be,
Like Hafez, from the world itself
    And from my soul set free . . .   I will arise.

And though I'm old, if you'll embrace
   Me tightly in your arms all night,
Then from your side, as dawn appears,
   Young in the morning light,   I will arise.

Flirtatious games, and youth,
   And wine like rubies glowing;
Convivial company,
   And drink that's always flowing;

A sweet-mouthed boy to serve
   And sweet-voiced singers too,
An elegant, dear friend
   Who's seated next to you;

A kindly youngster whose
   Delightful purity
Would stir the Fount of Youth
   To angry jealousy –

A stealer of men's hearts
   Whose charm and loveliness
Would make the moon herself
   Turn pale and envious;

A meeting place as though
   Heaven's high courts surround us,
With paradise's roses
   Profusely growing round us;

Kind-hearted friends to drink with,
   Servants who act discreetly,
Companions who keep secrets,
   Whom we can trust completely;

With wine as red as roses,
   Astringent, light to sip,
Whose tale is garnets, rubies,
   Kissed in a lover's lip;

The server's glance to be
   A sword to plunder reason,
The lovers' curls like snares
   To trip hearts with their treason;

A wit like Hafez, all
   Sweet-talk and repartee,
A patron like Qavam,
   Whose generosity

Lights up the world . . . and may
   The man who turns away
From pleasures such as these
   Not know one happy day!

With wine beside a gently flowing brook – this is best;
Withdrawn from sorrow in some quiet nook – this is
     best;
Our life is like a flower's that blooms for ten short days,
Bright laughing lips, a friendly fresh-faced look – this is
     best.

1. BOCCACCIO · *Mrs Rosie and the Priest*
2. GERARD MANLEY HOPKINS · *As kingfishers catch fire*
3. *The Saga of Gunnlaug Serpent-tongue*
4. THOMAS DE QUINCEY · *On Murder Considered as One of the Fine Arts*
5. FRIEDRICH NIETZSCHE · *Aphorisms on Love and Hate*
6. JOHN RUSKIN · *Traffic*
7. PU SONGLING · *Wailing Ghosts*
8. JONATHAN SWIFT · *A Modest Proposal*
9. *Three Tang Dynasty Poets*
10. WALT WHITMAN · *On the Beach at Night Alone*
11. KENKŌ · *A Cup of Sake Beneath the Cherry Trees*
12. BALTASAR GRACIÁN · *How to Use Your Enemies*
13. JOHN KEATS · *The Eve of St Agnes*
14. THOMAS HARDY · *Woman much missed*
15. GUY DE MAUPASSANT · *Femme Fatale*
16. MARCO POLO · *Travels in the Land of Serpents and Pearls*
17. SUETONIUS · *Caligula*
18. APOLLONIUS OF RHODES · *Jason and Medea*
19. ROBERT LOUIS STEVENSON · *Olalla*
20. KARL MARX AND FRIEDRICH ENGELS · *The Communist Manifesto*
21. PETRONIUS · *Trimalchio's Feast*
22. JOHANN PETER HEBEL · *How a Ghastly Story Was Brought to Light by a Common or Garden Butcher's Dog*
23. HANS CHRISTIAN ANDERSEN · *The Tinder Box*
24. RUDYARD KIPLING · *The Gate of the Hundred Sorrows*
25. DANTE · *Circles of Hell*
26. HENRY MAYHEW · *Of Street Piemen*
27. HAFEZ · *The nightingales are drunk*
28. GEOFFREY CHAUCER · *The Wife of Bath*
29. MICHEL DE MONTAIGNE · *How We Weep and Laugh at the Same Thing*
30. THOMAS NASHE · *The Terrors of the Night*
31. EDGAR ALLAN POE · *The Tell-Tale Heart*
32. MARY KINGSLEY · *A Hippo Banquet*
33. JANE AUSTEN · *The Beautifull Cassandra*
34. ANTON CHEKHOV · *Gooseberries*
35. SAMUEL TAYLOR COLERIDGE · *Well, they are gone, and here must I remain*
36. JOHANN WOLFGANG VON GOETHE · *Sketchy, Doubtful, Incomplete Jottings*
37. CHARLES DICKENS · *The Great Winglebury Duel*
38. HERMAN MELVILLE · *The Maldive Shark*
39. ELIZABETH GASKELL · *The Old Nurse's Story*
40. NIKOLAY LESKOV · *The Steel Flea*

41. HONORÉ DE BALZAC · *The Atheist's Mass*
42. CHARLOTTE PERKINS GILMAN · *The Yellow Wall-Paper*
43. C.P. CAVAFY · *Remember, Body . . .*
44. FYODOR DOSTOEVSKY · *The Meek One*
45. GUSTAVE FLAUBERT · *A Simple Heart*
46. NIKOLAI GOGOL · *The Nose*
47. SAMUEL PEPYS · *The Great Fire of London*
48. EDITH WHARTON · *The Reckoning*
49. HENRY JAMES · *The Figure in the Carpet*
50. WILFRED OWEN · *Anthem For Doomed Youth*
51. WOLFGANG AMADEUS MOZART · *My Dearest Father*
52. PLATO · *Socrates' Defence*
53. CHRISTINA ROSSETTI · *Goblin Market*
54. *Sindbad the Sailor*
55. SOPHOCLES · *Antigone*
56. RYŪNOSUKE AKUTAGAWA · *The Life of a Stupid Man*
57. LEO TOLSTOY · *How Much Land Does A Man Need?*
58. GIORGIO VASARI · *Leonardo da Vinci*
59. OSCAR WILDE · *Lord Arthur Savile's Crime*
60. SHEN FU · *The Old Man of the Moon*
61. AESOP · *The Dolphins, the Whales and the Gudgeon*
62. MATSUO BASHŌ · *Lips too Chilled*
63. EMILY BRONTË · *The Night is Darkening Round Me*
64. JOSEPH CONRAD · *To-morrow*
65. RICHARD HAKLUYT · *The Voyage of Sir Francis Drake Around the Whole Globe*
66. KATE CHOPIN · *A Pair of Silk Stockings*
67. CHARLES DARWIN · *It was snowing butterflies*
68. BROTHERS GRIMM · *The Robber Bridegroom*
69. CATULLUS · *I Hate and I Love*
70. HOMER · *Circe and the Cyclops*
71. D. H. LAWRENCE · *Il Duro*
72. KATHERINE MANSFIELD · *Miss Brill*
73. OVID · *The Fall of Icarus*
74. SAPPHO · *Come Close*
75. IVAN TURGENEV · *Kasyan from the Beautiful Lands*
76. VIRGIL · *O Cruel Alexis*
77. H. G. WELLS · *A Slip under the Microscope*
78. HERODOTUS · *The Madness of Cambyses*
79. *Speaking of Siva*
80. *The Dhammapada*